COUNCIL *on*
FOREIGN
RELATIONS

I0026648

Council Special Report No. 87
September 2020

The Day After in Venezuela

Delivering Security and
Dispensing Justice

Paul J. Angelo

The Council on Foreign Relations (CFR) is an independent, nonpartisan membership organization, think tank, and publisher dedicated to being a resource for its members, government officials, business executives, journalists, educators and students, civic and religious leaders, and other interested citizens in order to help them better understand the world and the foreign policy choices facing the United States and other countries. Founded in 1921, CFR carries out its mission by maintaining a diverse membership, with special programs to promote interest and develop expertise in the next generation of foreign policy leaders; convening meetings at its headquarters in New York and in Washington, DC, and other cities where senior government officials, members of Congress, global leaders, and prominent thinkers come together with Council members to discuss and debate major international issues; supporting a Studies Program that fosters independent research, enabling CFR scholars to produce articles, reports, and books and hold roundtables that analyze foreign policy issues and make concrete policy recommendations; publishing *Foreign Affairs*, the preeminent journal on international affairs and U.S. foreign policy; sponsoring Independent Task Forces that produce reports with both findings and policy prescriptions on the most important foreign policy topics; and providing up-to-date information and analysis about world events and American foreign policy on its website, CFR.org.

The Council on Foreign Relations takes no institutional positions on policy issues and has no affiliation with the U.S. government. All views expressed in its publications and on its website are the sole responsibility of the author or authors.

Council Special Reports (CSRs) are concise policy briefs, produced to provide a rapid response to a developing crisis or contribute to the public's understanding of current policy dilemmas. CSRs are written by individual authors—who may be CFR fellows or acknowledged experts from outside the institution—in consultation with an advisory committee, and are intended to take sixty days from inception to publication. The committee serves as a sounding board and provides feedback on a draft report. It usually meets twice—once before a draft is written and once again when there is a draft for review; however, advisory committee members, unlike Task Force members, are not asked to sign off on the report or to otherwise endorse it. Once published, CSRs are posted on CFR.org.

For further information about CFR or this Special Report, please write to the Council on Foreign Relations, 58 East 68th Street, New York, NY 10065, or call the Communications office at 212.434.9888. Visit our website, CFR.org.

To submit a letter in response to a Council Special Report for publication on our website, CFR. org, you may send an email to publications@cfr.org. Alternatively, letters may be mailed to us at: Publications Department, Council on Foreign Relations, 58 East 68th Street, New York, NY 10065. Letters should include the writer's name, postal address, and daytime phone number. Letters may be edited for length and clarity, and may be published online. Please do not send attachments. All letters become the property of the Council on Foreign Relations and will not be returned. We regret that, owing to the volume of correspondence, we cannot respond to every letter.

CONTENTS

FOREWORD

Venezuela is by many measures a failed state. The policies of the Nicolas Maduro administration have triggered what is Latin America's most serious humanitarian, economic, and political crisis. On his watch, Venezuela's economy has imploded, with hyperinflation and a poverty rate of 96 percent. In addition, the country has descended into lawlessness. Some five million Venezuelans have fled their homeland, threatening the capacity and stability of neighboring countries. Those who remain are often unable to feed themselves or purchase essential medicines. Meanwhile, two rival administrations claim to govern the country, with the United States and nearly sixty other countries recognizing opposition leader Juan Guaido as the constitutional leader, while China, Cuba, Russia, and others maintain relations with Maduro's regime.

In response to Maduro's moves to gut Venezuela's democratic institutions, and in an attempt to force him from power, the United States has levied sanctions on the country. This approach seemed to be making some headway, and an April 2019 uprising represented the most formidable domestic challenge to Maduro yet. Through a combination of handouts, proceeds from drug trafficking, repression, a mixture of Chinese, Russian, Cuban, and Iranian support, and the fragmentation and weakness of the opposition, however, Maduro has maintained power. It is impossible to predict if he will be forced to relinquish it any time soon.

In this Council Special Report, Paul Angelo, a fellow for Latin America studies at the Council on Foreign Relations, argues that although the United States might not know when a transition from Maduro could occur or the context in which it could happen, it must nonetheless prepare for that day. The United States will want to be ready to work with its partners to help Venezuela avoid disorder and support a new government that seeks to restore Venezuela's democracy. It is one thing for an illiberal regime to be ousted or fall, quite something else to ensure that something better and enduring takes its place.

Given the violence that has plagued Venezuela for years, Angelo argues that the most pressing task for a transitional government and its supporters would be to establish order. This would require co-opting the military, encouraging most military officials to join a transitional government, demobilizing local armed groups, retraining police forces, and prosecuting those members of the security services who are responsible for egregious abuses. The United States, for its part, would have to lift sanctions against those military officials who were to join a transitional government.

After providing security for its people, a transitional government should focus on restoring the rule of law and rehabilitating the country's judicial system. This would entail enticing judges and lawyers who had fled the country to return, removing abusive and corrupt judges and prosecutors, and revising the criminal code. Importantly, Angelo argues the transitional government should establish a truth commission, which would look into abuses committed during the Maduro regime, hear specific cases, sentence criminals, and award reparations. He also recommends that Venezuelan authorities dispense with retribution in favor of restorative justice and alternative sentencing, which could incentivize regime officials and military officers to defect and support a democratic transition.

Angelo offers a range of policy prescriptions for the United States that he argues would increase the chances that Venezuela's transition would be peaceful, orderly, and democratic. He asserts the United States needs to first and foremost build trust with Venezuelans, many of whom have grown up around the narrative that the United States is a malign actor. The United States should condition its support on the transitional government following a democratic path and should provide sanctions relief and participate in the country's reconstruction as long as leadership in Caracas exhibits a commitment to democracy and relieving human suffering. The United States should also assist the transitional government in cracking down on transnational gangs and drug traffickers that operate in Venezuela. For the present, Angelo recommends that the United States extend humanitarian aid to Venezuela and its neighbors, which have borne the brunt of the Venezuelan migrant and refugee crisis. He urges the United States and its partners to negotiate directly with potential spoilers such as China and Russia, providing reassurances that their economic interests will be protected in exchange for their cooperation during the transition.

What happens the day after Maduro leaves the political scene will do much to determine Venezuela's future and the complexion of the region for years to come. One can imagine a path of anarchy and conflict, where Venezuela continues to be a hotbed of violence and narco-trafficking and its people continue to flee the country. One can also imagine a successor regime coming to power that is not materially better than what currently exists. Another path, however, is brighter: one where Venezuela gradually restores its democracy, once again becomes one of the richest countries in Latin America, and renews its partnership with the United States. To make this third and incomparably more optimistic future more likely, the United States would be wise to adopt many of the policy recommendations outlined in this report.

Richard N. Haass
President
Council on Foreign Relations
September 2020

ACKNOWLEDGMENTS

I am grateful to Dr. Rebecca Bill Chavez and the members of the advisory committee for their time and input. The committee's insights were crucial in helping me dissect the complexity of Venezuela's crisis. I also thank CFR President Richard N. Haass, Senior Vice President and Director of Studies James M. Lindsay, Vice President and Deputy Director of Studies Shannon K. O'Neil, Senior Fellow and Director of the Center for Preventive Action Paul B. Stares, Editorial Director Patricia Dorff, Associate Editor Sumit Poudyal, Senior Manager Radmila Jackovich, and my research associate, David Gevarter. Their wisdom and feedback strengthened the content and recommendations of this report.

Paul J. Angelo

INTRODUCTION

Venezuela has fallen far from its storied place as the wealthiest country in South America. It is now the center of the largest humanitarian and political crisis in modern Latin American history, and some five million migrants and refugees have fled their ravaged homeland. Once seen as a paragon of political stability on the continent, Venezuela has all but collapsed, as parallel presidential administrations compete to provide government services to a beleaguered and divided citizenry.

The Barack Obama and Donald J. Trump administrations ratcheted up sanctions against the corrupt and abusive Nicolas Maduro administration, which has usurped Venezuela's democratic institutions and has overseen one of the biggest economic contractions in Latin American history.[1] Since January 2019, U.S. policy toward Venezuela has centered on Maduro's removal. The United States has advocated for a transitional government to facilitate a return to democracy.[2]

Maduro has thus far been resilient to diplomatic censure and economic sanctions. Short of military action, which would prove unpopular both in the United States and Venezuela, the United States has few tools to induce a transition from outside. Additional economic penalties are unlikely to provoke Maduro's downfall, as European governments have been slow to join U.S.-led sanctions and U.S. adversaries have managed to evade them.[3] The regime's involvement in drug trafficking and gold mining has also provided a steady source of illicit financing to Maduro and his deputies. If anything, sanctions relief, combined with specialized judicial processes, could help generate support for a transition from within the regime, especially from the military, which is characterized by factionalism.[4] Importantly, spelling out terms of transitional justice that are acceptable to the opposition coalition and are consistent with international law could convince pivotal regime officials to renounce Maduro.

Even though the circumstances under which a transition would happen are uncertain, the United States and other like-minded nations should prepare for that day. The coronavirus pandemic has further exposed the Venezuelan regime's incompetence, as healthcare infrastructure has deteriorated and food supplies have grown scarce. Oil sanctions and malfeasance have pushed the country's production to the lowest levels since 1945, crippling Venezuela's economy.[5] A combination of domestic discontent, international pressure, and the military's betrayal of Maduro could lead to regime change, and if abrupt, Maduro's departure could result in a contested transition and widespread disorder and unrest. During the Arab Spring, the United States and its allies were caught off guard by chaotic transitions in the Middle East and North Africa, and the lessons of those events suggest that in a country like Venezuela early international cooperation, including a stabilization plan, would be necessary to ensure a promising "day after."

Venezuela matters because the advent of an unstable autocratic regime in a region characterized by decades of democratic rule paves the way for illiberal governance and instability elsewhere in the Americas. Moreover, extra-regional powers such as China and Russia, which compete economically and diplomatically with the United States, have ties to Maduro that afford them a strategically important foothold in the Western Hemisphere.

Given Washington's insistence on Maduro's ouster, the U.S. government would be expected to assist Venezuelans if a transition occurs. The United States has already signaled its support for structural reforms to Venezuela's economy and humanitarian assistance for its citizens. Quickly establishing public order and reinstating the rule of law would be crucial for that support to be effective. And only after it has revived institutions to credibly deliver security and dispense justice could Venezuela restore democratic governance.

To this end, U.S. strategy in Venezuela should focus on generating trust with the Venezuelan people through robust aid, neutralizing external forces that benefit from the status quo, and promoting democracy through a multilateral approach. Working with other countries and international organizations would help offset suspicions created by a history of U.S. interventionism. Because the coronavirus pandemic stands to constrain international fiscal support, the United States should guide the hemispheric response and facilitate international cooperation to help Venezuelan security institutions establish a monopoly of force and to rehabilitate a judicial system damaged by decades of executive overreach.

FROM COOPERATION TO CRISIS
The Deterioriation of U.S.-Venezuela Relations

The United States and Venezuela enjoyed close ties for most of the twentieth century, particularly following the boom in Venezuela's oil production in the 1920s. Venezuela's anticommunist stance during the Cold War made it an important U.S. ally in the hemisphere, and its regular and peaceful elections reassured the United States at a time when most Latin Americans lived under authoritarian rule. But Venezuela's participatory system permitted only limited representation, and the country's two main parties monopolized political power for decades under an agreement known as the Punto Fijo pact.

U.S.-Venezuela relations took a turn for the worse after Hugo Chavez won the presidency in 1998.[6] A socialist firebrand, Chavez accused the political oligarchy of corruption and unseated Venezuela's traditional parties in a landslide.[7] During his first year in office, Chavez cooled to military cooperation with the United States, canceling the arrival of a U.S. Navy ship dispatched to aid Venezuelans during flooding that killed tens of thousands. His open embrace of Cuban head of state Fidel Castro created additional friction.[8] Even so, counternarcotics cooperation between Washington and Caracas persisted, as Venezuela remained an important outpost to monitor cocaine shipments from neighboring Colombia.[9]

Chavez's populism took a steady toll on Venezuela's democracy. A 1999 referendum resulted in a new constitution that extended extraordinary powers to the executive.[10] After a faction of the military failed to depose him in 2002, Chavez promoted his supporters in the military, assailed the independent media, and purged the state oil company of political opponents. The global rise in oil prices fueled Chavez's socialist transformation of Venezuela and facilitated redistributive economic policies, which proved instrumental to his reelection in 2000, 2006, and 2012.[11]

Despite the widespread perception that the George W. Bush administration had endorsed the coup attempt, Venezuela's diplomatic relations with the United States continued, albeit more warily.[12] Chavez and his United Socialist Party of Venezuela (PSUV) meanwhile pursued a closer relationship with U.S. adversaries—defending Iran's nuclear ambitions, investing in Russian defense equipment, and borrowing heavily from China. When oil prices collapsed in 2014, Venezuela's geopolitical realignment provided economic benefits, which became pivotal to the PSUV's electoral success after Chavez's death from cancer in 2013.

His handpicked successor, Nicolas Maduro, narrowly defeated the candidate of the opposition coalition, the Democratic Unity Roundtable (MUD), in the 2013 presidential election. When the MUD staged mass protests against electoral irregularities, Maduro suppressed them.[13] Under Maduro, the military's role in governance became increasingly prominent. Despite institutional rivalries within the security sector, Maduro ensured the compliance of senior military officers by rewarding them with cabinet and gubernatorial posts and by ignoring their involvement in drug trafficking. The prosperity of many military officers today is tied directly to Maduro's grip on power.

The *Chavista* assault on checks and balances also continued unabated. The MUD won a supermajority in the National Assembly in 2015 and sought to limit Maduro's overreach. However, the Supreme Tribunal of Justice, Venezuela's highest court, which is dominated by PSUV loyalists, suspended the legislature's powers in 2017.[14] The court also ordered a military tribunal to try the new judges appointed by the National Assembly for allegedly usurping constitutional authorities, forcing them into exile. And in its most brazen move, the high court permitted pro-Maduro parties to establish an entirely new quasi-legislative body known as the Constituent National Assembly.[15]

When the opposition coalition boycotted a 2018 presidential contest claiming repression, Maduro handily won reelection, which was plagued by gross irregularities and rejected by the National Assembly.[16] Invoking the constitutional succession clause, the National Assembly's current president, opposition leader Juan Guaido, assumed executive duties as interim president of Venezuela in January 2019 within weeks of Maduro's own inauguration ceremony. However, the National Assembly's inability to wrest control of the instruments of government, including the military, from Maduro has resulted in parallel diplomatic and administrative claims to Venezuela's executive branch and competing legislatures and judiciaries.

Almost sixty countries, including the United States, recognize Guaido as the constitutional leader. Some have joined U.S. sanctions against regime operatives.[17] Notwithstanding this support, the opposition lacks the financial and security resources to sideline Maduro, and the opposition coalition's internal divisions, which have thwarted its ability to win elections in the past, threaten to resurface as the country creeps toward a new elections deadline in December 2020.

A POLITICAL TRANSITION
Risks and Opportunities

Maduro continues to hold on to power through a combination of hand-outs, repression via security forces, Chinese and Russian economic and diplomatic support, and Cuban and Iranian intelligence cooperation.[18] Nonetheless, his removal remains a priority for Venezuela's democratic opposition and its international allies, which are counting on a combination of international pressure, social unrest, military discontent, and negotiations to unseat Maduro.

The first half of 2020 saw a notable increase in protests, particularly over gas and electricity shortages and declining humanitarian indicators.[19] Under Maduro, the poverty rate increased to 96 percent.[20] Despite repression, the number of monthly protests doubled from March to May, signaling growing desperation among the population. If conditions continue to decline, Maduro's trusted advisors, who recognize that the PSUV's domestic legitimacy depends on its ability to administer basic public services, could choose to replace him with a more competent leader or government.

Further, the Venezuelan security forces are not a monolith, and some senior leaders could determine that a coup is the only way to protect their interests.[21] Former regime officials claim that that up to 90 percent of troops oppose Maduro but fail to act out of fear.[22] The opposition coalition has already assured regime operatives of their inclusion in a transitional government and promised amnesty for security personnel who defect from Maduro and support a constitutional transition. During an abortive April 2019 uprising, the head of Maduro's intelligence police secretly negotiated his desertion with the opposition in exchange for safe passage out of the country and the lifting of U.S. sanctions against him.[23] Backdoor deals could convince similarly placed military officers to abandon Maduro and support a return to the constitutional order. Moreover, a public discussion of transitional justice measures, including immunity from criminal prosecution, could reassure enough members of Maduro's inner circle and the military, leading to decisive defections.

If popular mobilization and conspiracy inside the regime are insufficient, Maduro and the opposition coalition could resume formal negotiations, leading to an internationally brokered resolution to the political stalemate. UN-facilitated informal talks between Maduro and the opposition coalition in early 2020 led to a humanitarian agreement over the distribution of coronavirus relief assistance to the health sector. The enhanced presence of international actors in Venezuela to address the humanitarian crisis could help create diplomatic space for renewed dialogue that could then lead to a transition. Under these circumstances, the United States could consider sanctions relief to elicit major political concessions from the regime's negotiators.

Regardless of how the power transfer occurs, the best-case scenario—and one that the United States endorses in its "Democratic Transition Framework for Venezuela"—would be a provisional government replacing Maduro and overseeing the transition to fresh presidential and legislative elections.[24] U.S. policymakers would need to anticipate the fallout from a transition, even under the most auspicious conditions, and identify opportunities to ensure that the transitional context begets the restoration of democracy.

A democratic process would require participation of the PSUV and the opposition, as well as governors and mayors, civil society, and the country's military and police forces. A transition that brings Venezuela's major power brokers to the negotiating table would help ensure a lasting peace, the legitimacy of reforms to state institutions, and the restoration of democratic governance. Parties to the transition should make every effort to avoid the mistakes of the Punto Fijo pact, which excluded selected ideological movements from the national political life and set the stage for the country's present instability.

Transitions elsewhere suggest some common, predictable challenges that would need to be met. The immediate aftermath of Maduro's departure could see conflict among armed factions, unstable political coalitions, incentives for corruption and criminality, a divided international response, and an outflow of migrants and refugees. Venezuela is already one of the world's most dangerous countries—a place where common criminals and regime operatives extort, torture, and kill by the tens of thousands per year. The transitional government's legitimacy—and longevity—would hinge on successfully managing these threats to public order and citizen security while addressing the demands of the Venezuelan people for justice.

Given the complexity and scale of Venezuela's crisis, the magnitude of U.S. and other international contributions to restoring security and justice in Venezuela would likely exceed other recent international stabilization efforts.[25] In an era of tightened purse strings, though, the United States, European Union (EU), and international organizations would have to coordinate financial burden-sharing. Because a transition could come at any time, the United States should begin preparing now for the financial, political, and diplomatic challenges it may face in supporting the stabilization of a post-Maduro Venezuela.

STABILIZING THE SECURITY ENVIRONMENT
Establishing a Monopoly on Force

Political and criminal violence has accompanied Venezuela's constitutional crisis, and the first priority for the transitional government and its international supporters would be to stabilize the security environment. Venezuela has had the world's highest homicide rate three years in a row.[26] Further, state security forces killed nearly eighteen thousand people between 2016 and 2019 in instances of alleged "resistance to authority," prompting the International Criminal Court to open an initial inquiry into the systematization of extrajudicial murder.[27]

Although urban violence contributes to the lion's share of homicides, Venezuela's countryside and border regions are areas in continuous dispute, as control over illegal gold-mining operations and smuggling routes has proved lucrative in a country where the minimum wage dropped to a mere $2 per month in 2019.[28] Trafficking in contraband petroleum, drugs, arms, precious metals, and migrants is commonplace. Criminals often conduct their illegal activities with the complicity—and at times protection—of state forces in exchange for tribute.

As of February 2020, at least twenty-eight illegal armed groups operated along the porous Colombia-Venezuela border, including Colombian insurgent groups such as the National Liberation Army (ELN), dissident bands of the Revolutionary Armed Forces of Colombia (FARC), and organized crime outfits such as Venezuela's feared *sindicatos* and *pranes*.[29] Chavez and Maduro also armed a decentralized network of militia members, numbering at least 1.6 million, and PSUV-sponsored paramilitary groups known as *colectivos*, which count as many as 100,000 members within their ranks.[30] The colectivos, many of which are responsible for abuses against Venezuelan citizens, represent one of the principal challenges to peace-building in Venezuela.

CO-OPTING THE MILITARY

The opposition coalition's recovery roadmap, Plan País, pledges to steady the economy, address humanitarian concerns, and rebuild public services, but beyond general prescriptions for police and prison reform, it does not address the immediate security challenges that would intensify as state and nonstate actors alike angle for power and privilege.[31] Plan País unambiguously prescribes co-option of the National Bolivarian Armed Forces of Venezuela (FANB), which would remain the best guarantor of the constitutional order and the keeper of the peace throughout the transition.[32] However, the FANB's history of major corruption and abuse could complicate international cooperation and undermine popular trust in the institution.

Although Chavez and Maduro politicized the military, the U.S. government recognizes that the FANB would prove a strategic asset in Venezuela's transition and reconstruction.[33] The FANB's institutional memory and cohesion are essential to its ability to respond to Venezuela's security challenges. In Iraq, purging members of Saddam Hussein's Baath party from state institutions, especially the security forces, gutted those bodies of their expertise, corporate identity, and standards of professionalism, exacerbating the country's insecurity. Such a strategy is likely to create similar problems in Venezuela. At a minimum, the United States and its allies would have to relax sanctions enforcement against military officials who join the transitional government and support a return to democracy; to do otherwise would not only risk losing leverage over them but also make a transition less likely.[34]

Military personnel responsible for egregious abuses, such as extrajudicial murder and sexual violence, need to be removed from the institution and face justice under international human rights law. Doing so would also enhance the credibility of the FANB among Venezuelans. However, punitive action alone would be insufficient to maintain a professional force and separate guilty parties. As in Nicaragua during its transition from a socialist dictatorship to a democracy in 1991, financial inducements could be necessary to entice corrupt military leadership into retirement or to elicit their compliance.[35]

Likewise, internal divisions among the military's branches have increased during Maduro's rule, and the Venezuelan government would have to implement measures to prevent the FANB from fracturing. Chile long offered such institutional assurances by earmarking 10 percent of national copper revenues for the armed forces.[36] The Venezuelan government could contemplate similar arrangements between the FANB and the country's gold mines and oil fields. In addition to quelling dissent, a generous and steady budget would be necessary to finance a period of professionalization and institutional reform.

NEUTRALIZING ARMED GROUPS

The decentralization of Venezuela's security providers poses a major obstacle to consolidating law and order. In addition to the army, navy, air force, national guard, and national militia, formal security providers include the national police, state and municipal police, and the colectivos. The civilian forces have chains of command separate from the FANB and are also complicit in the regime's crimes and abuses. These nonmilitary groups exert social control locally, which they would be reticent to relinquish. A transitional government would need to revamp and retrain police forces at each level of government. However, some subnational and local forces that are the cause of much local insecurity should be subdued and replaced by the FANB until new state and municipal police forces can be reconstituted.

The transitional government would have to define which subnational police, militias, colectivos, and criminal organizations it seeks to co-opt and retrain, which it seeks to demobilize, and which it seeks to prosecute. As in Honduras during a recent police reform, a special investigative commission comprising civil society leaders could oversee purging the most predatory individuals and units, especially those engaged in extrajudicial murders.[37] Because crimes such as homicide and kidnapping fuel citizen perceptions of insecurity, any such commission and state security operations would need to target groups that exhibit the most violent behavior early on. Given the capacity limitations of the FANB, though, Venezuelan authorities would have to sequence their consolidation of armed control by focusing first on cities, where most of the population resides, and then turning their attention to the countryside.

Illegal armed groups, some of which have ties to state security forces, pose additional challenges. Regrettably, mafia dons and warlords would be important to keeping Venezuela stable during the initial phases of the transition. As with corrupt members of the FANB, striking power-sharing deals that are mutually advantageous for the Venezuelan government and nonstate groups could be necessary. This provisional tactic would be at odds with the broader strategy of building democracy. Messaging from the transitional government and its international partners should manage expectations about the timeline for the full restoration of democratic governance while maintaining confidence and momentum in the process.

CREATING OPPORTUNITIES FOR INTERNATIONAL ASSISTANCE

Notwithstanding the supremacy of the FANB, other state security forces and paramilitary groups in some areas would generate friction as the Venezuelan army encroaches on the de facto prerogatives of regional and municipal police forces.[38] The presence of an impartial international body would help prevent partisan or factional violence by supporting an inclusive political process and by verifying the implementation of a timeline to restore government services, address the humanitarian crisis, and hold elections. The United Nations is suited to perform this role, as the UN Charter provides a legal basis for sustained peacekeeping intervention via the Security Council.[39]

A robust UN special political mission would be preferable to a peacekeeping mission. Whereas some stabilization missions (e.g., in Haiti) assign policing duties to UN troops due to a lack of professional state security forces, security provision in Venezuela should remain the responsibility of national security forces, which possess the personnel and infrastructure to be effective. The UN mission's scope and design would be driven by the law-and-order conditions on the ground, but assuming the cohesion of state security forces, the UN Mission in Colombia (2016–2017) and the UN Verification Mission in Colombia (2017–present) are a good, albeit imperfect, model. The United Nations' activities fused a traditional political mission with aspects of interim stabilization by employing unarmed international observers to monitor a cease-fire, ensure the collective security of demobilizing FARC insurgents, and oversee the reintegration of ex-combatants.[40]

In Venezuela, UN officials could support the transitional government's dialogue with the country's armed groups, manage the logistics of their disarmament, and introduce community violence reduction programming. As the country moves from the transitional phase toward elections, the government would provide considerable incentives for militias and colectivos to participate in a disarmament, demobilization, and reintegration process overseen by the United Nations and observed by the International Committee of the Red Cross, two organizations that have cooperated on disarmament in other countries. The Organization of American States (OAS) could complement the United Nations' work as it did during the successful demobilization and resettlement of the Nicaraguan Contras from 1989 to 1993. Given the unity of some factions of the militias and colectivos, the Venezuelan government would do well to maintain their community-based structures after disarmament and, with the help of international organizations, retrain them as civilian service corps to staff state reconstruction projects or disaster response.

A UN special representative would periodically verify implementation of political and security agreements that would pave the way for a return to democratic governance, and UN activities would focus on rebuilding trust between the Venezuelan people and the FANB by verifying reforms to the security forces, monitoring human rights, and securing uncontrolled arms. The UN Observer Mission in El Salvador, for example, helped that country reintegrate tens of thousands of ex-combatants, dismantle its abusive police force, rebuild its courts, and administer elections after twelve years of civil war.

As in El Salvador, the UN High Commissioner for Refugees would have a major role in repatriating millions of Venezuelans and providing protection to returning asylum seekers. During the coronavirus pandemic, many Venezuelans abroad have lost their jobs owing to economic downturn. Colombia's recent experience in facilitating the return of tens of thousands of migrants to Venezuela through subsidized busing provides a rudimentary yet effective template for how to tackle the relocation of so many people amid health and security crises. To keep this movement from destabilizing the transitional government and jeopardizing an already fragile security environment, the United Nations and international donors would need to fund regional governments and local civil society organizations to orchestrate a phased, orderly return of migrants.

A lack of access to affordable and nutritious food is at the heart of Venezuela's humanitarian crisis, as one in every three Venezuelans is food insecure.[41] State and nonstate actors alike have used food to build patronage networks in Venezuela. Given its logistical reach and history of civic action, the FANB would likely remain involved in humanitarian aid distribution in the immediate aftermath of a transition, but the administration of food aid in particular should quickly shift to international organizations and civil society.[42] The UN World Food Program (WFP) could work with local nongovernmental organizations to identify gaps in coverage and then surge emergency assistance to communities left behind.[43] The WFP and other donors could also strike agreements with Venezuela's private sector and existing commercial grocery networks to relieve the government of the logistical challenges associated with supplying food nationwide and, importantly, to depoliticize food distribution.

ADDRESSING UNFRIENDLY FOREIGN INFLUENCE

Beyond Venezuela's armed criminals, Maduro's international allies could disrupt or even sabotage a Western-led stabilization mission. Venezuela is a principal axis along which great power competition with China and Russia plays out in the Western Hemisphere and even at the United Nations. Maduro has mortgaged the Venezuelan oil sector to China and Russia in exchange for generous loans and political support. Cuba, Iran, and Turkey have also expanded their economic and diplomatic ties with Maduro, securing energy resources and gold.[44] Relieving Venezuela's debt obligations, most likely with an International Monetary Fund (IMF) cash infusion and aggressive debt forgiveness, would have to be a priority. Although it is up to the Venezuelan transitional government to manage its relations with U.S. competitors, a constructive relationship between the transitional government and the United States and other democracies through generous security and development assistance would ensure a basis for democratic reforms.

China could prove more amenable to cooperation with a transitional government than the United States' other geopolitical competitors. Venezuela owes Chinese creditors as much as $20 billion, and Beijing has a vested interest in ensuring the Venezuelan government's stability and financial viability.[45] However, Russia would likely retain strong ties to elements of Venezuela's security forces, the extent of which would depend on how effectively other countries exert their influence. The Venezuelan armed forces depend on the Russian government for arms sales and maintenance, so the United States and its allies would need to make institutional inroads by identifying equipment and training gaps and then enticing the FANB into security cooperation agreements to address those deficiencies.[46]

Maduro has deep ties to Havana, but many FANB leaders distrust the Cuban officials who have embedded with the Venezuelan security forces and propped up the regime through counterintelligence operations.[47] The Cuban government could plausibly retain a presence in Venezuela if the PSUV participates in the transitional government, but Cuba stands to lose some influence—and possibly access to petroleum—in any power sharing that involves the opposition. Cuba could play a permissive role in Venezuela's transition but only if the new government in Caracas continued to sell cheap oil to Havana.

Notwithstanding its popularity among everyday Venezuelans, the United States' clout could diminish due to poor relations with the PSUV and U.S. adversaries.[48] Common hemispheric resolve would be the core facilitator of Venezuela's stabilization. By co-opting the FANB, prioritizing the disarmament of abusive state and nonstate actors, and resolving food security, the United States, its regional and other Western allies, and the United Nations stand a good chance of helping the Venezuelan state deliver its most fundamental obligation to its people: their security.

THE RULE OF LAW AND TRANSITIONAL JUSTICE
The Balance Between Accountability and Reconciliation

Given the scale of abuse and criminality that has taken place under the PSUV's rule, a critical responsibility of Venezuela's transitional government would be to restore the rule of law and the government's ability to dispense justice. Rule of law requires that all citizens have equal access to justice through established and legitimate legal procedures, while ensuring that all individuals, including the agents of the state, remain equally accountable to the law. In its absence, democracy cannot thrive.

The Chavez and Maduro governments have undermined the rule of law by politicizing the courts, criminalizing activism, and authorizing arbitrary detentions. In 2017, the International Commission of Jurists declared that Venezuela's judicial branch had ceased to be an "independent and impartial organ of public authority."[49] The country's high court, packed with PSUV supporters, has usurped the National Assembly; extended dominant powers to the executive branch; and failed to prosecute Maduro and his loyalists for human rights abuses, public corruption, and infiltration by organized crime. At least 40 percent of criminal court judges are publicly supportive of the PSUV, and more than 460 former judges signed lucrative business deals with the regime.[50] In response, the opposition-controlled National Assembly staffed a parallel Supreme Tribunal of Justice in exile to document abuses and deliver indictments for Maduro and his deputies in absentia.

In addition to rebuilding an independent judiciary, Venezuela would require specialized laws and procedures for dealing with abuses committed during the authoritarian period. Transitional justice paradigms include a mixture of prosecution, truth seeking, reparations, and a guarantee of non-repetition through institutional reform. The ultimate goal is to prevent further conflict by delivering accountability and addressing the causes of rights violations.[51]

Venezuela is obligated to comply with international legal requirements in this regard, but the volatility of transitional contexts often creates an irreconcilable tension between what a state should do and what it can do. The pressure to sacrifice retribution for peace and order led to blanket amnesty for human rights abusers in Chile and Argentina, and justice only came from high courts decades later.[52] Venezuelan authorities should be prepared to balance the pursuit of justice with the political imperative of keeping regime loyalists committed to a democratic transition. Restorative justice, especially the use of alternative sentencing that emphasizes reparations over imprisonment, could be a critical facilitator of both social peace and reconciliation, which are necessary for Venezuela's stability. If the opposition coalition and its international supporters make such a commitment to alternative sentencing now, it could even hasten the defection of regime officials and military officers and thereby encourage a transition.

REFORMING AGENTS OF THE LAW

The transitional government needs to stop ongoing human rights abuses, including civilian trials in military courts, and release all political prisoners in the state's custody. The triad of law and order—the security forces, the courts, and the penal system—should be the focus of Venezuela's restoration of the rule of law. Venezuela's police are famously corrupt, and elite forces such as the Special Action Force and the Bolivarian Intelligence Service have been implicated in some of the regime's worst abuses. The FANB should aim to transfer its internal security role to civilian police forces eventually, but those agencies need to undergo reform. Similarly, the country's prison system perpetuates impunity, as criminals continue to operate their networks from behind bars. The OAS's Department of Public Security is well poised to parlay the experiences of other countries in the hemisphere to inform the design of investigative training, human rights instruction, and penitentiary overhaul in Venezuela. Additionally, the OAS could help the Venezuelan government implement vetting protocols for police officers, intelligence officials, and prison staff.

Rebuilding Venezuela's judiciary would also require massive investments in the institution's workforce. Nearly two decades of politicization has gutted the judiciary, as many of the country's top legal professionals have fled the country. Enticing these individuals to return and participate in judicial reform through subsidies and tax incentives would be an essential task for the transitional government. The transitional government should also direct a conduct-based evaluation of the judiciary and remove abusive judges and prosecutors.

If Venezuela failed to guarantee the independence of its courts from the earliest stages of the transition, the government's broader work in restoring democratic governance could be discredited.[53] Likewise, although many state agents are complicit in Maduro's crimes, not all security and justice personnel are criminals; differentiating between the two would help build confidence in the transitional government and maintain a vigorous corps of jurists and legal staff.

STRENGTHENING THE JUDICIARY THROUGH INTERNATIONAL ASSISTANCE

From the outset, Venezuela's transitional government should emphasize strengthening the technical capacity of its courts. Judges, prosecutors, and law professors should revise the criminal code to remove abusive and unjust statutes introduced during the authoritarian period while investigative police and prosecutors build new cases through evidence collection and witness interviews.[54]

The United States could support judicial reform in Venezuela through new training opportunities and technical assistance. The American Bar Association (ABA) Rule of Law Initiative has for two decades partnered with judiciaries, attorneys, and law schools in the Americas to introduce regional anti-trafficking statutes, provide recommendations for criminal code reforms, and implement forensics training. As it has in other countries in Latin America, the U.S. Agency for International Development (USAID) could fund a multiyear ABA assistance mission in Venezuela aimed at retraining, professionalizing, and certifying the country's legal professionals.

Affording Venezuela's neighbors a role in the transition is also vital considering the degree to which they have been affected by cross-border criminal activity and migrant flows. OAS member states have little recent experience in regional security or stabilization missions, but many possess significant technical expertise in rehabilitating justice sectors. The OAS Mission to Support the Fight Against Corruption and Impunity in Honduras (MACCIH) investigated networks of public and private corruption that remained beyond the reach of local judicial authorities due to inexperience, corruption, or intimidation.[55] Likewise, the United Nations sponsored a similar and successful intervention known as the International Commission Against Impunity in Guatemala (CICIG), which embedded international investigators with national prosecutors to bring cases in front of national courts.[56] The United States and other Western nations could encourage the Venezuelan transitional government to authorize an international anti-impunity mission that harnesses the recent experiences of the OAS and the United Nations.

ENABLING TRANSITIONAL JUSTICE

As judicial independence is reestablished, Venezuela would need to conduct a census of human rights violations. In the absence of a national narrative of the country's political crisis—one that is acceptable to the major power brokers—transitional justice risks becoming a mechanism that enables either impunity or revenge, neither of which will build the legitimacy or credibility of incipient judicial bodies. To avoid these pitfalls, the transitional government would have to establish a truth commission, staffed by Venezuelan civil society and supported by international observers.

Defining the parameters of the commission would be an important task, one for which the Office of the UN High Commissioner for Human Rights (OHCHR) and the OAS Inter-American Commission on Human Rights have expertise. Both organizations operate mechanisms to monitor human rights abuses in Venezuela and have tracked closely the mounting violations in recent years.[57] UN and OAS oversight would ensure that "gross violations of human rights or humanitarian law, including violations which were part of a systematic pattern of abuse," do not escape consideration and would give the truth commission the credibility to work on behalf of victims.[58] The OHCHR could help guide the process by recommending or even appointing, as Venezuelan law permits, international commissioners to the body, as was done in Sierra Leone, El Salvador, and Guatemala.[59]

Following the compilation of testimonies, the Venezuelan government could establish a transitional justice tribunal to hear cases, assign responsibility, sentence criminals, and administer reparations. Due process and fair trial protections would be essential to the tribunal's credibility, but blanket amnesty for serious crimes remains a violation of Venezuela's obligations under international human rights law.[60] Equally, the U.S. government would request extradition only for crimes not covered under the transitional justice process and after defendants have completed any sentences for human rights violations—a clear demonstration of support for the tribunal's credibility.

Colombia's implementation of the FARC peace process included both a truth commission and a special tribunal. The special tribunal is rooted in the principles of restorative justice, delivering sanctions such as community service to offenders in exchange for honest confessions, forfeiture of illicit assets, and support for reparations. In fact, the FARC agreed to disarm and demobilize only on the condition that they would not face prison sentences under the ordinary criminal justice system.[61]

Similar judicial guarantees could convince enough members of the FANB to abandon Maduro, who protects the security forces from prosecution in exchange for their loyalty. Blanket amnesty, as has been floated by the opposition coalition, would risk violating international law and the country's own constitution.[62] Restorative justice, on the other hand, would be consistent with international law, provide assurances that regime operatives could take seriously, and incentivize the FANB's participation in a transition. Although some Venezuelans could view alternative sentencing as impunity, such measures allow perpetrators to confront and remedy harm for all but the most heinous atrocities while affirming the dignity of victims and repairing the country's social fabric.[63] A credible restorative justice system would, above all, help set the country on a course toward social peace and reconciliation.

RECOMMENDATIONS

Whether the "day after" would abide by the terms set out by the United States' "Democratic Transition Framework for Venezuela" is unknowable. Nevertheless, the U.S. government's close relationship with the opposition coalition and Venezuelan civil society—not to mention its resources to help rebuild the country—would ensure that Washington retains some leverage to shape Venezuela's transition. And despite differences in opinion about how to achieve a transition in Venezuela, U.S. commitment to democracy promotion in Venezuela has consistently garnered bipartisan support. Leading Democrats and Republicans recognize that helping Venezuela resolve its political, economic, and humanitarian crises is in the interest of the United States and its partners in the Americas. To achieve this end, the U.S. government should prioritize the following strategies.

BUILD TRUST WITH VENEZUELANS

The United States should focus first on activities aimed at building trust with the Venezuelan authorities and people. An entire generation of Venezuelans has grown up knowing only a government that has maligned the U.S. legacy in Venezuela, and the PSUV would continue to exert a prominent influence in most transitional scenarios. U.S. authorities should condition their support on the transitional government's commitment to a democratic transition and to alleviating humanitarian suffering, while seeking points of entry that engender goodwill and create opportunities for deeper U.S. involvement in the country's reconstruction. Sanctions relief for some PSUV and military officials and the country's oil and defense sectors would be a necessary step.

Furthermore, U.S. intelligence and law enforcement agencies should assist the Venezuelan transitional government in thwarting transnational criminality, a top concern for everyday Venezuelans and U.S. citizens alike. The United States and others seeking to assist would need a detailed understanding of the power brokers in major urban areas and lawless rural zones in Venezuela. The U.S. government's Place-Based Strategy in Central America offers a promising model for reducing violence in marginalized city neighborhoods.[64] And as the U.S. intelligence community helped Colombia during that country's struggle against the FARC insurgency, geospatial mapping resources to detail the operating areas of illegal armed groups would be critical to targeting criminal activities elsewhere.

Additionally, the U.S. government should appeal to the Venezuelan people through expanded humanitarian aid now and by restarting economic development work in Venezuela once a transition occurs. USAID should fund local resilience programs to help those facing chronic poverty and recurrent food crises. In addition, the United States should sponsor members of the Venezuelan diaspora who live in the United States to participate in humanitarian brigades aimed at rebuilding the country. As in the Balkans, USAID should likewise back the sale of diaspora bonds to finance development projects and should create a platform to link members of the diaspora with citizens in Venezuela to provide access to credit and capital for small- and medium-sized enterprises—a critical source of poverty relief.

CREATE DISINCENTIVES FOR POTENTIAL SPOILERS

In addition to working through the United Nations and OAS, the U.S. government should negotiate with potential spoilers of the transition outside Venezuela. China's wish to guarantee debt repayment would incentivize its cooperation with whatever government results from the transition. Transitional authorities should provide reassurances that they intend to honor China's financial interests in Venezuela. The United States should further encourage partners in the Americas that have strong ties to China (e.g., Argentina, Brazil, Chile, and Peru) to solicit China's support for a democratic transition in Venezuela.

The United States should respect any transitional government decisions to honor Russia's investments in Venezuela but should actively counterbalance Russian influence by partnering with institutions that do not have close ties to Moscow. Agencies and executive offices at national and subnational levels run by members of the current opposition coalition should be the initial priority. Additionally, the U.S. Department of Defense should work toward opening an Office of Security Cooperation in Venezuela and encourage Venezuelan attendance at the Inter-American Defense Board and College. The FANB has lacked professional training for decades, and many within its ranks would be eager to learn from the world's leading militaries. Because elements of the FANB are suspicious of the United States, the Pentagon should work with Canada and the EU to emphasize defense institution–building to improve the FANB's internal governance and to press for the FANB's publication of a citizen security strategy. The U.S. government resumed security cooperation activities with Ecuador in 2018 after leftist President Rafael Correa halted military-to-military contacts in 2014; U.S. authorities should make a similar appeal to Venezuela's transitional government.[65]

Soliciting Cuban support—or at least acquiescence—would oblige a return to dialogue with the Cuban government. The United States and Cuba have previously found common cause on fighting drug trafficking and human smuggling, and a more constructive relationship between Washington and Havana would improve chances of success in Venezuela.[66] Even in the absence of constructive bilateral relations, Washington should encourage trusted partners that have friendlier diplomatic relations with Cuba, such as Canada and Spain, to facilitate information sharing to disrupt transnational criminal networks.

RELY ON INTERNATIONAL PARTNERSHIPS

As the largest shareholder at the World Bank and IMF, Washington would certainly be involved in Venezuela's debt restructuring, but its role in helping restore security and justice to Venezuela is more ambiguous. Accordingly, the U.S. government should use its relationships with other governments in the hemisphere and in Europe that have sustained less hostile relations with Maduro to ensure that international assistance has a multilateral brand. The credibility of the United Nations' and OAS's work in Venezuela would depend every bit as much on the breadth of multilateral participation as it would on the depth of expertise.

Venezuela's immediate neighbors, especially Colombia and Brazil, would seek to play a role in helping repatriate refugee populations and in combating cross-border criminality. Countries such as Argentina, Chile, Portugal, and Spain possess the historical experience to be useful guides for security and justice sector reform following authoritarianism. The U.S. government should join them in contributing to the efforts of international organizations to help Venezuela depoliticize its law-and-order institutions. Similarly, Mexico's and Argentina's insistence on maintaining their neutrality in Venezuela's political crisis and Costa Rica's long history of peacemaking in the region could make them critical facilitators in a democratic transition.

As it did for Haiti, the United States should host a donor conference to fund a multilateral stabilization mission in Venezuela. North American and European contributions would be critical in light of severe economic contraction in Latin America and the Caribbean in 2020.[67] To ensure the sustainability of security and justice improvements, the United States should also aim to be a top provider of assistance to UN and OAS activities through the State Department's Global Peace Operations Initiative.[68] U.S. foreign assistance under Plan Colombia (2000–2011) amounted to more than $8 billion and serves as an important reference for the kind of investment required to help put Venezuela on the right path. Just as the United States was a top donor to the MACCIH and the CICIG but did not micromanage the operation of either body, so too should it support security and justice initiatives by international organizations in Venezuela without creating the perception of asserting too heavy a hand.

CONCLUSION

Maduro will leave behind a legacy of oppression, economic ruin, and raging insecurity. Whether post-Maduro Venezuela devolves into anarchy and conflict, like Afghanistan, or follows the path to full democracy, like Chile, will depend on how Venezuelan authorities and its international partners manage the transition in its earliest days. Addressing the corruption and mismanagement of the Venezuelan state will require delivering sanctions relief, resolving food insecurity, fostering democratic elections, reigniting the oil sector, and bringing an end to one of the world's largest refugee crises.

However, stabilizing the security environment and rebuilding the judiciary are two critical areas in which little planning has been done. They are also challenges that the United States, Venezuela's neighbors, and international organizations could help resolve. The security, humanitarian, and economic fallout of inaction would otherwise have enormous reputational and strategic costs for the United States and its democratic partners. Indeed, no matter the circumstances of the transition, the United States should once again raise its flag above its embassy in Caracas, and its diplomats and policymakers should work tirelessly for the cause of democracy in Venezuela. Only then would the terms of "the day after" reassure Venezuelans that their best days are ahead of them.

ENDNOTES

1. Gideon Long, "Venezuela Data Offer Rare Glimpse of Economic Chaos," *Financial Times*, May 29, 2019, http://ft.com/content/5cb83c1c-821b-11e9-b592-5fe435b57a3b.

2. Tom Phillips, "Venezuela Elections: Maduro Wins Second Term," *Guardian*, May 21, 2018, http://theguardian.com/world/2018/may/21/venezuela-elections-nicolas-maduro-wins-second-term; and Anthony Faiola and Carol Morello, "U.S. Proposes Transitional Government for Venezuela, Without Maduro or Guaido," *Washington Post*, March 31, 2020, http://washingtonpost.com/world/the_americas/us-proposes-transitional-government-for-venezuela-without-maduro-or-guaido/2020/03/31/8642a99a-7352-11ea-ad9b-254ec99993bc_story.html.

3. Joshua Goodman, "Report: New Players Help Maduro Evade Tanker Sanctions," *Washington Post*, July 13, 2020, http://washingtonpost.com/national/report-rogue-tankers-help-maduro-evade-sanctions/2020/07/13/d2b86eea-c4fb-11ea-a825-8722004e4150_story.html.

4. Joshua Goodman, "Venezuela's Maduro Cracks Down on His Own Military in Bid to Retain Power," *New York Times*, August 13, 2019, http://nytimes.com/2019/08/13/world/americas/venezuela-military-maduro.html.

5. Fabiola Zerpa, "Venzuela's Oil Production Plunges to Lowest Level Since 1945," Bloomberg, June 12, 2020, http://bloomberg.com/news/articles/2020-06-12/venezuela-s-oil-production-plunges-to-lowest-level-since-1945.

6. Fabiana Sofia Perera and John Polga-Hecimovich, "U.S.-Venezuelan Relations Under Chavismo," in *U.S.-Latin American Defense Relations*, ed. Craig Deare (unpublished manuscript, September 12, 2019), 2.

7. Gerver Torres, "The Venezuelan Drama in 14 Charts," Center for Strategic and International Studies, January 16, 2019, http://csis.org/analysis/venezuelan-drama-14-charts.

8. Jose de Cordoba, "The Future of 'Cubazuela,'" *Wall Street Journal*, March 1, 2013, http://wsj.com/articles/SB10001424127887323884304578328252463429328.

9.   K. Larry Storrs, *Drug Certification/Designation Procedures for Illicit Narcotics Producing and Transit Countries*, RL32038 (Washington, DC: Congressional Research Service, September 20, 2005), 10.

10. John Polga-Hecimovich, "Bureaucratic Politicization, Partisan Attachments, and the Limits of Public Agency Legitimacy: The Venezuelan Armed Forces Under Chavismo," *Latin American Research Review* 54, no. 2 (2019): 476–98, http://larrlasa.org/articles /10.25222/larr.142.

11. Although elected initially in 1998, Chavez sought to "re-legitimate" his presidency under the terms of the 1999 constitution and called for a new presidential contest in 2000. With each successive election, Chavez nationalized the country's major industries and took steps to censor the press, thus stifling his political opponents. See Laura Neuman and Jennifer McCoy, *Observing Political Change in Venezuela: The Bolivarian Constitution and 2000 Elections* (Atlanta, GA: Carter Center, February 2001), http://cartercenter.org/documents/297.pdf.

12. Christopher Marquis, "Bush Officials Met With Venezuelans Who Ousted Leader," *New York Times*, April 16, 2002, http://nytimes.com/2002/04/16/world/bush-officials -met-with-venezuelans-who-ousted-leader.html.

13. Forty-three people were killed, eight hundred were injured, and the MUD's top leadership was imprisoned. See Clare Ribando Seelke et al., *Venezuela: Background and U.S. Relations*, R44841 (Washington, DC: Congressional Research Service, March 12, 2020), 4. The MUD ceased to be an organizing body for the opposition coalition in 2018. This report refers to the main anti-Maduro parties as the opposition coalition. See also "New Opposition Front Launched," *Economist*, March 12, 2018, http:// country.eiu.com/article.aspx?articleid=1686511952&Country=Venezuela&topic =Politics&subtopi_7.

14. The opposition's victory in the 2015 parliamentary election reflected growing disenchantment with Chavismo in Venezuela and gave the MUD a democratic mandate that served as the basis for Juan Guaido's interim presidency claim. See Alejandro Salinas Rivera and Federico Andreu-Guzman, *The Supreme Court of Justice of Venezuela: An Instrument of the Executive Branch* (Geneva: International Commission of Jurists, August 2017), 3–4, http://icj.org/wp-content/uploads/2017/09/Venezuela -Suprem-Court-Publications-Reports-Thematic-reports-2017-ENG.pdf.

15. Leila Miller, "Venezuelan Judges Work From Abroad and Await Maduro's Ouster," *Los Angeles Times*, May 7, 2019, http://latimes.com/world/la-fg-venezuela-supreme-court -judges-20190507-story.html.

16. Jose Ignacio Hernandez, "Rigged Elections: Venezuela's Failed Presidential Election," *Electoral Integrity Project*, May 30, 2018, http://electoralintegrityproject.com /international-blogs/2018/5/30/rigged-elections-venezuelas-failed-presidential-election.

17. Despite European support for Guaido, the U.S. Department of the Treasury has opened investigations into transactions between Spain's central bank and the Maduro regime that potentially violate U.S. sanctions. Moreover, given Spain's financial interests, the Spanish government blocked the European Union from implementing sectoral sanctions against Venezuela, instead opting for targeted ones against regime officials. See Martin Arostegui, "Risk of U.S. Sanctions Looms as Venezuela Roils

Spanish Election," Voice of America, November 5, 2019, http://voanews.com/europe
/risk-us-sanctions-looms-venezuela-roils-spanish-election.

18. Seelke et al., *Venezuela: Background and U.S. Relations*, 6.

19. "Conflictividad Social Primer Semestre 2020," Observatorio Venezolano de
Conflictividad Social, June 2020, http://observatoriodeconflictos.org.ve/oc/wp
-content/uploads/2020/07/INFORMEOVCS-PRIMERISEMESTRE2020-1.pdf.

20. Bibi Borges, "How Maduro Is Using COVID-19 to Silence His Opponents Even
Further," *Americas Quarterly*, July 21, 2020, http://americasquarterly.org/article
/how-maduro-is-using-covid-19-to-silence-his-opponents-even-further.

21. Frank O. Mora, "Stabilizing Venezuela: Scenarios and Options," Council on Foreign
Relations, June 14, 2019, http://cfr.org/report/stabilizing-venezuela.

22. John Otis, "Venezuela's Army Remains Supportive of President Maduro," NPR, March
21, 2019, http://npr.org/2019/03/21/705395155/venezuelas-army-remains-supportive
-of-president-maduro.

23. Anthony Faiola, "Maduro's Ex-Spy Chief Lands in U.S. Armed With Allegations
Against Venezuelan Government," *Washington Post*, June 24, 2019, http://
washingtonpost.com/world/the_americas/maduros-ex-spy-chief-lands-in-us-armed
-with-allegations-against-venezuelan-government/2019/06/24/b20ad508-9477-11e9
-956a-88c291ab5c38_story.html.

24. Democratic Transition Framework for Venezuela," Department of State, March 31,
2020, http://state.gov/democratic-transition-framework-for-venezuela.

25. The annual budget for seven UN peacekeeping missions in Africa reached more than
five billion dollars, to which the United States contributed more than one-fifth of the
total sum in 2019. See Luisa Blanchfield, Lauren Ploch Blanchard, and Alexis Arieff,
UN Peacekeeping Operations in Africa, R45930 (Washington, DC: Congressional
Research Service, September 23, 2019), 8.

26. Lucia Newman, "Venezuela Has 'World's Highest Murder Rate,'" Al Jazeera, January
23, 2020, http://aljazeera.com/news/2020/01/venezuela-worlds-highest-murder-rate
-200123135543539.html.

27. "Venezuela: Extrajudicial Killings in Poor Areas," Human Rights Watch, September
18, 2019, http://hrw.org/news/2019/09/18/venezuela-extrajudicial-killings-poor-areas;
and "Statement of the Prosecutor of the International Criminal Court, Fatou Bensouda,
on Opening Preliminary Examinations Into the Situations in the Philippines and in
Venezuela," International Criminal Court (ICC), February 8, 2018, http://icc-cpi.int
/Pages/item.aspx?name=180208-otp-stat.

28. Hector Pereira Caracas, "Venezuelan Minimum Wage Hits Rock Bottom: $2.00 a
month," Agencia EFE, August 31, 2019, http://efe.com/efe/english/world/venezuelan
-minimum-wage-hits-rock-bottom-2-00-a-month/50000262-4053749.

29. *Sin Dios ni Ley, Un Análisis de la Situación de Seguridad en la Frontera Colombo-
Venezolana* [Without God or Law, An Analysis of the Security Situation on the
Colombian-Venezuelan Border] (Fundación Paz & Reconciliación, February 2020),
7, http://pares.com.co/wp-content/uploads/2020/02/INFORME-DE-SEGURIDAD
-EN-LA-FRONTERA-1.pdf.

30. Luke Taylor, "Maduro Turns to Violent 'Mercenary' Colectivos to Maintain Order," *The World*, April 25, 2019, http://pri.org/stories/2019-04-25/maduro-turns-violent-mercenary-colectivos-maintain-order.

31. "Stabilizing Venezuela"; and *Plan País: Political Agreement to Free Venezuela From Social Crisis and Economic Collapse*, December 2019, 11–12, http://db1fe89e-8172-4a44-804c-6aae6df8a86a.filesusr.com/ugd/002151_d96949b2274143479dc214ea21095431.pdf.

32. *Plan País*, 12; and James Dobbins et al., *The Beginner's Guide to Nation-Building* (Santa Monica, CA: RAND Corporation, 2007), xx, http://rand.org/pubs/monographs/MG557.html.

33. "Democratic Transition Framework for Venezuela."

34. Rather than repeal the sanctions regulation itself, the U.S. government should delist those who cooperate with democratic leadership and no longer pose a threat to U.S. national security. Leaving the sanctions in place has the benefit of allowing the United States to relist individuals who fail to follow through on their commitments. See "The United States Sanctions Venezuela's Defense and Security Sector," U.S. Department of State, May 10, 2019, http://state.gov/the-united-states-sanctions-venezuelas-defense-and-security-sector.

35. The FANB has 2,000 admirals and generals—almost twice as many what the U.S. military has. Bloating at the top of the organization should be relieved by enticing those who are not removed under criminal or disciplinary procedures into retirement. See Brian Ellsworth and Mayela Armas, "The Maduro Mystery: Why the Armed Forces Still Stand by Venezuela's Beleaguered President," Reuters, July 28, 2019, http://reuters.com/investigates/special-report/venezuela-military. Lee Hockstader, "Sandinista Handouts Stir Bitter Row in Nicaragua," *Washington Post*, June 23, 1991, http://washingtonpost.com/archive/politics/1991/06/23/sandinista-handouts-stir-bitter-row-in-nicaragua/07c2cdb2-537d-4f79-95ad-fa12feed9fc5.

36. Jonathan Kandell, "Chile—An Embarrassment of Riches," *Institutional Investor*, December 19, 2017, http://institutionalinvestor.com/article/b150nxlwjtm11y/chile-an-embarrassment-of-riches.

37. Despite purging more than 5,000 members of the Honduran National Police, the Special Purge and Transformation Commission failed to build successful judicial cases against criminal officers ousted from the force. Some purged officers continued to operate crime rings with impunity. It was not until three years after the Commission's inauguration that the Honduran government created a complementary elite police force to prosecute former police officers involved in crime. See David R. Dye, "Police Reform in Honduras: The Role of the Special Purge and Transformation Commission," Wilson Center, June 2019, http://wilsoncenter.org/sites/default/files/media/documents/publication/lap_dye_police-english_final.pdf.

38. The FANB leadership has historically valued social peace and internal cohesion. However, the institution's politicization under Chavez and Maduro accentuated interservice rivalries, generational rifts, and socioeconomic tensions. Flag officers' political loyalty to the PSUV and their access to the spoils of the kleptocratic regime have put them at odds with midrange officers, many of whom are loyal to the constitution, and junior officers, most of whom were raised under a training system that conflated military training with political indoctrination.

39. The OAS could play a similar role in the United Nations' absence, but the OAS's recognition of the opposition coalition as the constitutional authority in Venezuela and repeated denunciation of Maduro's assault on democracy have discredited the organization among PSUV leadership, whose buy-in would be necessary in most likely transitional scenarios. See Aditi Gorur, *Defining the Boundaries of UN Stabilization Missions* (Washington, DC: Stimson Center, December 2016), http://stimson.org/wp-content/files/file-attachments/Defining-Boundaries-UN-Stabilization-Missions.pdf.

40. "Mandate," UN Verification Mission in Colombia, accessed May 27, 2020, http://colombia.unmissions.org/en/mandate.

41. "WFP Venezuela Food Security Assessment: Main Findings; Data Collected Between July and September 2019," World Food Program (WFP), February 23, 2020, http://reliefweb.int/report/venezuela-bolivarian-republic/wfp-venezuela-food-security-assessment-main-findings-data.

42. Iselin Asedotter Stronen, "'A Civil-Military Alliance': The Venezuelan Armed Forces Before and During the Chávez Era," CMI Working Paper 4, Chr. Michelson Institute, Bergen, May 2016, http://cmi.no/publications/5808-a-civil-military-alliance.

43. As the World Food Program has piloted in Jordan with Syrian refugees, the UN agency should eventually transition to using biometric data and blockchain technology to avoid fraud and overhead costs while authenticating regular and equitable food distribution to needy populations. See Maddie Seibert, "The World Food Program: Fighting Hunger With Blockchain," Foodtank, January 2019, http://foodtank.com/news/2019/01/the-world-food-program-fighting-hunger-with-blockchain.

44. Mircely Guanipa and Deisy Buitrago, "Venezuela Receives Material From Iran to Help Restart Refinery–Official," Reuters, April 23, 2020, http://reuters.com/article/us-venezuela-oil-iran/venezuela-receives-material-from-iran-to-help-restart-refinery-official-idUSKCN2253FX.

45. Alicia Hernandez, "China Remains Quiet and Pragmatic on Venezuela Crisis," Dialogo Chino, January 20, 2020, http://dialogochino.net/en/trade-investment/32971-china-remains-quiet-and-pragmatic-on-venezuela-crisis.

46. The U.S. government pursued such a strategy in Mexico in light of the Mexican army's reluctance to work closely with the United States, and following a surge of U.S. security assistance, the Mexican navy scored some of the country's most prominent operational successes against organized crime.

47. Angus Berwick, "Special Report: How Cuba Taught Venezuela to Quash Military Dissent," Reuters, August 22, 2019, http://reuters.com/article/us-venezuela-cuba-military-specialreport/special-report-how-cuba-taught-venezuela-to-quash-military-dissent-idUSKCN1VC1BX.

48. Santiago Perez, "Trump, Unpopular Elsewhere, Has Lots of Fans in Venezuela," *Wall Street Journal*, March 6, 2019, http://wsj.com/articles/trump-widely-disparaged-abroad-has-lots-of-fans-in-venezuela-11551882601.

49. Rivera and Andreu-Guzman, *The Supreme Court of Justice of Venezuela*.

50. Ofelia Riquezes and Frank O. Mora, "Transitional Justice and the Democratic Transition Framework for Venezuela," Global Americans, May 7, 2020, http://

theglobalamericans.org/2020/05/transitional-justice-and-the-democratic-transition-framework-for-venezuela.

51. *Guidance Note of the Secretary-General: United Nations Approach to Transitional Justice* (New York: United Nations Rule of Law Unit, March 2010), 3, http://un.org/ruleoflaw/files/TJ_Guidance_Note_March_2010FINAL.pdf.

52. In Uruguay, a plebiscite following the transition resulted in blanket amnesty for military officers who had committed abuses during the dictatorship. Although the process was democratic, the result betrayed democracy, as it failed to protect the individual rights of the military's victims.

53. South Africa serves as a warning to Venezuela: despite having transitioned to a postapartheid presidency, apartheid-era judges—all but three of whom were white males—retained their positions, including those who actively discriminated against defendants and were complicit in the government's abuses. See Tholakele H. Madala, "Rule Under Apartheid and the Fledgling Democracy in Post-Apartheid South Africa: The Role of the Judiciary," North Carolina Journal of International Law and Commercial Regulation 26, no. 3 (Summer 2001): 750–56.

54. Dobbins et al., *The Beginner's Guide to Nation-Building*, xxviii.

55. Although the OAS Mission to Support the Fight Against Corruption and Impunity in Honduras (MACCIH) uncovered major criminal rings, the country's attorney general, an executive appointee, retained the power to shelve or impede sensitive criminal investigations, ultimately enfeebling the body and prompting its closure in early 2020. See Charles T. Call, "International Anti-Impunity Missions in Guatemala and Honduras: What Lessons for El Salvador?," American University Center for Latin American and Latino Studies Working Paper Series no. 21, June 2019, 4–5, http://american.edu/centers/latin-american-latino-studies/upload/international-anti-impunity-missions-in-guatemala-and-honduras-what-lessons-for-el-salvador-rev4.pdf.

56. "Opinion Poll Shows That 72% of Guatemalan People Support CICIG'S Work," Comisión Internacional Contra la Impunidad en Guatemala (CICIG), April 5, 2019, http://cicig.org/citizen-support/opinion-poll-shows-that-72-of-guatemalan-people-support-cicigs-work/?lang=en.

57. "Human Rights in the Bolivarian Republic of Venezuela: Report of the United Nations High Commissioner for Human Rights on the Situation of Human Rights in the Bolivarian Republic of Venezuela," report no. A/HRC/41/18 (unedited advance version), United Nations High Commissioner for Human Rights, July 5, 2019, http://ohchr.org/en/NewsEvents/Pages/DisplayNews.aspx?NewsID=24788&LangID=E; and Inter-American Commission on Human Rights, "IACHR Establishes Special Follow-Up Mechanism for Venezuela (MESEVE)," press release no. 267/19, October 21, 2019, oas.org/en/iachr/media_centereleases/2019/267.asp.

58. *Rule-of-Law Tools for Post-Conflict States: Truth Commissions*, HR/PUB/06/1 (New York: Office of the United Nations High Commissioner for Human Rights, 2006), 9, http://ohchr.org/Documents/Publications/RuleoflawTruthCommissionsen.pdf.

59. *Rule-of-Law Tools for Post-Conflict States*, 14.

60. Claudio Grossman, "The Inter-American System of Human Rights: Challenges for the Future," *Indiana Law Journal* 83, no. 4 (Fall 2008): 1,276, http://ilj.law.indiana.

edu/articles/83/83_4_Grossman.pdf. Victims may push for the involvement of the International Criminal Court (ICC), but under the principle of complementarity, the ICC's Office of the Prosecutor need not act if the national judiciary is investigating or prosecuting the cases in question.

61. "Colombia: FARC Dicen que No Aceptarán Ir a La Cárcel Luego de Proceso de Paz," BBC, March 27, 2013, http://bbc.com/mundo/ultimas_noticias/2013/03/130327 _ultnot_farc_dicen_no_sugerencia_gobierno_paz_msd.shtml.

62. Mieczysław P. Boduszyński and Victor Peskin, "Guaidó Backed an Amnesty Plan for Venezuela's Military. How Might That Play Out?" *Washington Post*, February 11, 2019, http://.washingtonpost.com/news/monkey-cage/wp/2019/02/11/guaido-backed-an -amnesty-plan-for-venezuelas-military-how-might-that-play-out.

63. Martha Minow, "Do Alternative Justice Mechanisms Deserve Recognition in International Criminal Law? Truth Commissions, Amnesties, and Complementarity at the International Criminal Court," *Harvard International Law Journal* 60, no. 1 (Winter 2019), http://harvardilj.org/wp-content/uploads/sites/15/HILJ_601_1_Minow.pdf.

64. Jim Nealon, "The 'Place-Based Strategy' in Honduras," *Foreign Service Journal*, October 2018, http://afsa.org/place-based-strategy-honduras.

65. "Fact Sheet on Cooperation Between the United States and Ecuador," U.S. Mission Ecuador, Department of State, June 28, 2018, https://ec.usembassy.gov/fact-sheet-on -cooperation-between-the-united-states-and-ecuador.

66. Andrea Rodriguez and Michael Weissenstein, "US, Cuba Still Cooperating on Stopping Drug Smugglers," AP News, June 22, 2017, http://apnews.com /ec4e1a9ae56847fa9b1896fb48b5b027.

67. "COVID-19 to Cause Biggest Economic Contraction Ever in Latin America and Caribbean," UN News, April 21, 2020, http://news.un.org/en/story/2020/04/1062292.

68. Michael Smith and Jennifer Pulliam, "U.S. Support for Global Peacekeeping Operations," Foreign Press Centers Briefing, U.S. Department of State, May 28, 2019, http://state.gov/upcoming-u-s-support-for-global-peacekeeping-operations.

ABOUT THE AUTHOR

Paul J. Angelo is a fellow for Latin America studies at the Council on Foreign Relations (CFR). His work focuses on U.S.-Latin American relations, transnational crime, military and police reform, and immigration. Previously, Angelo was an international affairs fellow at CFR, and in this capacity, he represented the U.S. Department of State as a political officer at the U.S. Embassy in Tegucigalpa, Honduras, where he managed the ambassador's security and justice portfolio. As a U.S. naval officer, Angelo deployed to Colombia on three occasions over the course of more than a decade. During his longest mission in Colombia, he served as the U.S. Embassy's principal liaison to the Colombian military in the Pacific coast region. He was directly responsible for the planning of interagency missions focused on improving local governance, rule of law, and security in support of Plan Colombia. Angelo holds a BS in political science from the U.S. Naval Academy, where he was awarded the Truman Scholarship; an MPhil in Latin American studies from Oxford University, where he studied as a Rhodes Scholar; and a PhD in politics from University College London.

ADVISORY COMMITTEE
The Day After in Venezuela

Cynthia J. Arnson
Woodrow Wilson International Center for Scholars

Harriet C. Babbitt
National Democratic Institute

William Brownfield
Center for Strategic and International Studies

Michael J. Camilleri
Inter-American Dialogue

Rebecca Bill Chavez, *Chair*
Inter-American Dialogue

Fernando Cutz
Cohen Group

James F. Dobbins
RAND Corporation

Richard D. Downie
Delphi Strategic Consulting

Patrick D. Duddy
Duke University

Luigi R. Einaudi
National Defense University

Daniel P. Erikson
Blue Star Strategies

Mark B. Feierstein
Albright Stonebridge Group

Vanda Felbab-Brown
Brookings Institution

Benjamin N. Gedan
Woodrow Wilson International Center for Scholars

Juan Sebastian Gonzalez
Cohen Group

Steve Hege
U.S. Institute of Peace

This report reflects the judgments and recommendations of the author. It does not necessarily represent the views of members of the advisory committee, whose involvement should in no way be interpreted as an endorsement of the report by either themselves or the organizations with which they are affiliated.

J. Welby Leaman
Walmart

Jason Marczak
Atlantic Council

Thomas McNamara
Elliott School
of International Affairs

Johanna Mendelson-Forman
American University

Juan E. Mendez
American University

Sarah Deardorff Miller
Refugees International

Keith Mines
U.S. Institute of Peace

Fabiana Sofia Perera
William J. Perry Center
for Hemispheric Defense Studies

Annie Pforzheimer
Center for Strategic and
International Studies

John Polga-Hecimovich
U.S. Naval Academy

Celina B. Realuyo
National Defense University

Daniel Restrepo
Center for American Progress

Elizabeth Rosenberg
Center for a New American
Security

Andrew D. Selee
Migration Policy Institute

www.ingramcontent.com/pod-product-compliance
Lightning Source LLC
Chambersburg PA
CBHW070818280326
41934CB00012B/3219